50 SPANISH PHRASES

Catherine Bruzzone and Susan Martineau

Illustrations by Leighton Noyes
Spanish adviser: Rosa María Martín

Contents

Special note for learners!

The key Spanish phrases you will learn are numbered on each spread. There are also extra words you will need for the activities. By the end of the book you will know 50 SPANISH PHRASES and many useful Spanish words. There is a summary of all these at the back of the book.

Pronouncing Spanish

The simple pronunciation guide will help, but it cannot be completely accurate. Read the words as if they were English. Put the stress on the letters in *italics*, for example, ah-dee-*ohs*. If possible, ask for help from a Spanish-speaking person and try to speak on your own as soon as you can.

¡Hola!

Have fun saying hello and good-bye in Spanish.
You need to match the right greeting to the pictures, according to the time of day illustrated. Say the correct phrase out loud. You can check your answers on page 32.

1

Hola, buenos días
oh-lah *bweh*-nos *dee*-ahs
Hello, good morning

2

Adiós
ah-dee-*ohs*
Good-bye

3

Buenas tardes
bweh-nahs-*tar*-dehs
Good evening

4

Buenas noches
bweh-nahs *noch*-ehs
Goodnight

Words to Know	**Hasta luego**	**la tarde**
¡Hola!	*ahs*-tah loo-*eh*-go	lah *tahr*-deh
oh-la	See you soon	evening
Hi!		
	el día	**la noche**
	ehl *dee*-ah	lah *noch*-eh
	day	night

Me llamo,...

Ask your friends or family to play this naming game with you. One person needs to be blindfolded and spun around. Then he or she has to "find" someone and ask **¿Cómo te llamas?** The person answers **Me llamo...** and says **¿Y tú?** Take turns being the "finder." You could all choose a Spanish name!

5

¿Cómo te llamas?
koh-moh teh *yam*-ahs?
What's your name?

6

Me llamo,...
meh *yam*-oh
My name is,...

7

¿Y tú?
ee too
And you?

Choose a Name!

Juan
hoo-*ahn*

Carlos
kahr-lohs

José
hoz-*eh*

Francisco
frahn-*seess*-koh

María
mah-*ree*-ah

Pilar
peel-*ahr*

Silvia
sill-*vee-ah*

Isabel
eeza-*bell*

¿Cuántos años tienes?

You will need two dice for this game. One person throws them and the other asks **¿Cuántos años tienes?** The dice thrower answers **Tengo… años**, putting in the number the dice add up to. Take turns.

8

¿Cuántos años tienes?
koo-*ahn*-tohs *ahn*-yohs tee-*eh*-nehs
How old are you?

9

Tengo nueve años
tehn-goh noo-*eh*-veh *ahn*-yohs
I am nine years old

10

¡Feliz cumpleaños!
fel-*ees* koompleh-*ahn*-yohs
Happy birthday!

Numbers! Numbers!

1	**uno**	*oo*no		**7**	**siete**	see-*eh*-teh
2	**dos**	dohs		**8**	**ocho**	*och*-oh
3	**tres**	trehs		**9**	**nueve**	noo-*eh*-veh
4	**cuatro**	*kwah*-troh		**10**	**diez**	dee-*ess*
5	**cinco**	*seen*-koh		**11**	**once**	*on*-seh
6	**seis**	sayss		**12**	**doce**	*doh*-seh

Look at the numbers on the inside front cover if you want to ask some older people their ages!

¿Qué tal?

Cut out a circle of paper or card. Draw a smiley face on one side and a glum one on the other. Ask your friends **¿Qué tal?** as you show them one of the faces. They have to try to give the right answer depending on if it is smiley or glum. Swap around so that you can practice too.

11

¿Qué tal?
keh tal
How are you?

12

Bien, gracias
bee-en *gras*-ee-ahs
I'm fine, thanks

13

No estoy bien
noh ehs-*toh-ee* bee-*en*
I'm not so well

Words to Know

Así así
ah-*see* ah-*see*
So-so

Bastante bien
bas-*tan*-teh bee-*en*
Quite well

Muy bien
mwee bee-*en*
Very good

Muy mal
mwee mal
Awful

Gracias
grah-see-ahs
Thank you/thanks

¿Dónde está...?

Find all of the items in the **Words to Know** list and put them on a tray. Practice saying the Spanish words for them. Now close your eyes while a friend takes one item off the tray. (Cover up the Spanish words too.) You then have to ask **¿Dónde está el/la...?** whatever the missing thing is! Your friend will either say **Aquí está el/la...** or **¡Una vez más!** Take turns and try to remember.

14

¿Dónde está...?
dohn-deh ehs-*tah*
Where is,..?

15

Aquí está el/la,...
akee ehs-*tah* el/lah
Here is the,..

¡Una vez más!
*oo*na vehs mass
Try again!

A note about el and la
There are two words for "the" in Spanish – **el** and **la**.
Try to learn them when you learn a new noun.

Words to Know

el libro
el *lee*-broh
book

el lápiz
el *lah*-pees
pencil

el lápiz de color
el *lah*-pees deh ko*lor*
colored pencil

el pegamento
el pega-*men*-toh
glue

el papel
el pa-*pel*
paper

la pluma
lah *ploo*-ma
pen

la goma
lah *goh*-mah
rubber

la regla
lah *reh*-glah
ruler

¿Qué es esto?

Look at this outdoor scene and practice saying the Spanish words. Then ask some friends or your family to play a drawing game with you. You each take turns drawing one of the named items and ask **¿Qué es esto?** Everyone else has to try to say what it is from the drawing (and without looking at the Spanish words). They say **Es un/una....**

17

¿Qué es esto?
keh ehs *ehs*-toh
What is it?

una niña
*oo*na *neen*-yah
girl

una bicicleta
*oo*na beesee-*kleh*-tah
bicycle

un picnic
oon *peek*-neek
picnic

un pájaro
oon *pah*-hah-roh
bird

una pelota
*oo*na peh-*loh*-tah
ball

18

Es un/una,...
ehs *oon/oo*na
It's a,...

una mochila
*oo*na moh-*chee*-lah
backpack

un banco
oon *ban*-koh
bench

un niño
oon *neen*-yoh
boy

A note about *un* and *una*
There are two words for "a" in Spanish – **un** and **una**.
You say **es un** for an **el** word and **es una** for a
la word. For example, **es una niña** or **es un pájaro**.

13

Aquí está la familia

Spot the family! Look at page 15. Which four people are members of the same family? Point them out and say **Aquí está el hijo** or **Aquí está la hija**. Use other words from **Words to Know** with **Aquí está** too. When you have found the whole family, you can say **Aquí está la familia**. Check your answers on page 32.

19

Aquí está el hijo
ah-*kee* ehs-*tah* el *ee*-ho
Here's the son

20

Aquí está la hija
ah-*kee* ehs-*tah* lah *ee*-ha
Here's the daughter

21

Aquí está la familia
ah-*kee* ehs-*tah* lah fam-*ee*-lee-ah
Here's the family

Words to Know

la madre/mamá
lah *mah*-dreh/ma-*mah*
mother/mom

el padre/papá
el *pah*-dreh/pa-*pah*
father/dad

los padres
los *pah*-drehs
parents

la hermana
lah air-*mah*-na
sister

el hermano
el air-*mah*-no
brother

el bebé
el beh-*beh*
baby

la abuela
lah ah-*bweh*-lah
grandmother

el abuelo
el ah-*bweh*-loh
grandfather

Me gusta/me gustan...

Have a look at this picture and try and learn the Spanish words for everything. Then choose four things you like and four you don't like. Practice saying if you like them or not by using the phrases **Me gusta/me gustan…** and **No me gusta/no me gustan….** For example, **Me gusta el sol** and **Me gustan los árboles** or **No me gusta la lluvia** and **No me gustan los mosquitos**. Practice with a friend and take turns.

las cabras
lass *kab*-rahs
goats

los mosquitos
loss mohs-*keet*-ohs
mosquitos

23
No me gusta/
no me gustan...
noh meh *goos*-tah/
noh meh *goos*-tan
I don't like,..

la lluvia
lah *yoo*-vee-ah
rain

22
Me gusta/
me gustan,..
meh *goos*-tah/
meh *goos*-tan
I like,..

los conejos
loss kon-*ay*-hohs
rabbits

las flores
lass *flor*-ehs
flowers

los gatos
loss *gah*-tohs
cats

el sol
el sol
sun

los árboles
loss *ar*-bol-ehs
trees

los patos
los *pah*-tohs
ducks

los cerdos
loss *sair*-dohs
pigs

los perros
loss *pehr*-rohs
dogs

las arañas
lass ah-*rahn*-yahs
spiders

A Note About Me gusta/me gustan
There are two ways of saying "I like" in Spanish – **me gusta** and **me gustan**. You say **me gusta** when you like <u>one</u> thing and **me gustan** when you like more than one. For example, **Me gusta el sol** (I like the sun) or **Me gustan las flores** (I like flowers).

17

¿Dónde vives?

The children in the pictures are telling us where they live. Practice saying the phrases. Then cut out four pieces of paper to cover speech bubbles 25-28 and number them from 1 to 4. Ask a friend or adult to call out **uno**, **dos**, **tres** or **cuatro** and say **¿Dónde vives?** You have to try to remember how to say where you live according to the scene next to the number.

24

¿Dónde vives?
don-deh *vee*-vess
Where do you live?

25

Vivo en una casa
vee-vo en *oon*a *kah*-sah
I live in a house

26

Vivo en un departamento
vee-vo en oon deh-parta-*men*-toh
I live in an apartment

27

Vivo en la ciudad
vee-vo en lah see-oo-*dad*
I live in town

28

Vivo en el campo
vee-vo en el *kam*-poh
I live in the country

Quiero,..

Have some fun with this Spanish shopping game for two or more people. Look at the shopping list and practice the words. The first player says **Quiero manzanas, por favor,** and then points at the next thing on the list, the strawberries, on the market stall. The next player has to add them to the phrase, saying **Quiero manzanas y fresas, por favor**.
Each player adds another thing to the list and the winner is the first one to say the whole list correctly.
Then you can shout **Ya está, gracias.**

29
Quiero,...
kee-*air*-oh
I would like (some),...

30
Por favor
pohr fah-*vohr*
Please

31
Ya está, gracias
ya stah *gras*-ee-ahs
That's all, thanks

The Shopping List

manzanas
man-*sah*-nahs
(some) apples

fresas
fray-sahs
(some) strawberries

plátanos
plah-tah-nohs
(some) bananas

uva
oo-vah
(some) grapes

zanahorias
zanah-*or*-eeahs
(some) carrots

papas
pah-pahs
(some) potatoes

tomates
to-*mah*-tehs
(some) tomatoes

ensalada
ensah-*lah*-dah
(some) salad/lettuce

Un vaso de agua, por favor

It's time to eat, so try asking for food and drink in Spanish. You can ask a friend or adult to say **¿Qué quieres?** All you need to do is choose something tasty from the menu and add **por favor**. You might also like to say **Tengo hambre** or **Tengo sed**.

Un vaso de agua,
por favor
oon *vah*-so deh *ag*-wah pohr fah-*vohr*
A glass of water,
please

Menu/El menú el men-*oo*

un jugo de naranja
oon *hoo*go deh nah-*ran*-hah
an orange juice

un vaso de agua
oon *vah*-so deh *ag*-wah
a glass of water

un vaso de leche
oon *vah*-so deh *leh*-cheh
a glass of milk

un trozo de pastel
oon *tro*-so deh pas-*tel*
a piece of cake

un yogur
oon yog-*oor*
a yogurt

fruta
froo-tah
fruit

pan
pan
bread

jamón
ham-*on*
ham

queso
keh-soh
cheese

papas fritas
pah-pahs *free*-tahs
potato chips

¿Qué quieres hacer?

You need two or more people to play this acting game. Read the phrases and then cover them up. One of you asks **¿Qué quieres hacer?** and acts out one of the activities. The other player, or players, answer **Quiero...** whatever they think the activity is. Take turns being the actor.

36

¿Qué quieres hacer?
keh kee-*air*-ehs ah-*sehr*
What do you want to do?

37

Quiero mirar la tele
kee-*air*-oh mee-*rar* lah *teh*-leh
I want to watch TV

38

Quiero jugar al fútbol
kee-*air*-oh hoo*gar* al *foot*-bol
I want to play soccer

39

Quiero ir en bicicleta
kee-*air*-oh eer en bee-see-*kleh*-tah
I want to ride a bike

40

Quiero nadar
kee-*air*-oh nad-*ar*
I want to go swimming

Words to Know

¿Quieres…?
kee-*air*-ehs
Do you want to…?

Sí, quiero
see kee-*air*-oh
Yes, I'd like to

No, gracias
noh *gras*-ee-ahs
No thanks

25

¿De qué color es?

Here's a fun game to help you practice colors in Spanish with your friends or family. You will need a die and some counters. When you land on a square all the other players shout **¿De qué color es?** You say **Mi color preferido es el rojo** or whatever color you have landed on. If you get the answer wrong you have to miss a turn. Good luck!

41

¿De qué color es?
deh keh kol-or ehs
What color is it?

START

FINISH

42

¿Cuál es tu color preferido?
kwal ess too kol-or preh-fair-ee-doh
What's your favorite color?

Count in Spanish as you move your counter.

43

Mi color preferido es el,...
mee kol-*or* preh-fair-*ee*-doh ess el...
My favorite color is,...

Colors/Los colores los kol-*or*-ehs

rojo	**verde**	**negro**	**anaranjado**
roh-ho	*vehr*-deh	*neh*-groh	anaran-*hah*-doh
red	green	black	orange
azul	**amarillo**	**blanco**	**marrón**
ah-*sool*	amah-*ree*-yoh	*blan*-koh	mah-*ron*
blue	yellow	white	brown

¿Adónde vas?

These children are all dressed for their vacations. See if you can match the right phrases to the children. Say **¿Adónde vas?** and then choose the right answering phrase. Practice saying this out loud too. Check your answers on page 32.

44

¿Adónde vas?
ah-*dohn*-deh vahs
Where are you going?

45

Voy a la playa
voy ah lah *plah*-yah
I'm going to the beach

46

Voy al campo
voy al *kam*-po
I'm going to the country

47

Voy a la montaña
voy ah lah mon-*tan*-yah
I'm going to the mountains

48

Voy a la ciudad
voy ah lah see-oo-*dad*
I'm going to town

Words to Know

de vacaciones
deh vakah-see-*on*-ess
on vacation

¡Buen viaje!
bwen vee-*ah*-heh
Have a good trip!

Me pongo

It's time to get dressed – in Spanish! Have a look at the first picture and say **Me pongo pantalones pequeños.** Now look at the second picture and describe the difference in the pants.
Say **Me pongo pantalones grandes.** Continue describing the differences between the clothes on page 31. You'll need to use the **Words to Know** and have a look at the **Big or Small?** note too.
You can check the answers on page 32.

49

Me pongo pantalones pequeños
meh *pon*-go panta-*loh*-nehs pek-*en*-yohs
I'm wearing small pants

50

Me pongo
pantalones grandes
meh *pon*-go panta-*loh*-nehs *gran*-dehs
I'm wearing
big pants

Big or Small?

If the noun you are describing is an **el** word, you use **un pequeño**. If the noun is a **la** word, you use **una pequeña**. For example, **un abrigo pequeño** or **una falda pequeña**. **Grande** stays the same.

If the words are plural (more than one) add an "**s**."
For example, **abrigos pequeños**, **faldas grandes**.

Words to Know

pantalones
panta-*loh*-nehs
pants

un abrigo
oon ab-*ree*-goh
a coat

una camiseta
*oo*na kamee-*say*-tah
a T-shirt

una gorra
*oo*na *gor*-rah
a cap

una falda
*oo*na *fal*-dah
a skirt

un suéter
oon *swet*-air
a sweater

**pequeño/
pequeña**
pek-*en*-yoh/pek-*en*-yah
small

grande
gran-deh
big

Las respuestas/Answers

Here are the answers to the activities on pages 2-3, 14-15, 28-29 and 30-31.

pages 2-3

4 Buenas noches

2 Adiós

1 Hola, buenos días

3 Buenas tardes

pages 14-15

Aquí está la madre/mamá

Aquí está el abuelo

Aquí está la hija/hermana

Aquí está el hijo/hermano

pages 28-29

47 Voy a la montaña

45 Voy a la playa

48 Voy a la ciudad

46 Voy al campo

pages 30-31

Me pongo un abrigo grande

Me pongo una camiseta grande

Me pongo una falda grande

Me pongo un suéter grande

Me pongo una gorra grande

Me pongo un abrigo pequeño

Me pongo una camiseta pequeña

Me pongo una falda pequeña

Me pongo un suéter pequeño

Me pongo una gorra pequeña

50 frases españolas/50 Spanish Phrases

1 **Hola, buenos días** Hello, good morning
2 **Adiós** Good-bye
3 **Buenas tardes** Good evening
4 **Buenas noches** Goodnight
5 **¿Cómo te llamas?** What's your name?
6 **Me llamo…** My name is…
7 **¿Y tú?** And you?
8 **¿Cuántos años tienes?** How old are you?
9 **Tengo nueve años** I am nine years old
10 **¡Feliz cumpleaños!** Happy birthday!
11 **¿Qué tal?** How are you?
12 **Bien, gracias** I'm fine, thanks
13 **No estoy bien** I'm not so well
14 **¿Dónde está…?** Where is…?
15 **Aquí está el/la…** Here is the…
16 **¡Una vez más!** Try again!
17 **¿Qué es esto?** What is it?
18 **Es un/una…** It's a…
19 **Aquí está el hijo** Here's the son
20 **Aquí está la hija** Here's the daughter
21 **Aquí está la familia** Here's the family
22 **Me gusta/me gustan…** I like…
23 **No me gusta/no me gustan…** I don't like…
24 **¿Dónde vives?** Where do you live?
25 **Vivo en una casa** I live in a house
26 **Vivo en un departamento** I live in an apartment
27 **Vivo en la ciudad** I live in town
28 **Vivo en el campo** I live in the country
29 **Quiero…** I would like…
30 **Por favor** Please
31 **Ya está, gracias** That's all, thanks
32 **¿Qué quieres?** What would you like?
33 **Tengo hambre** I'm hungry
34 **Tengo sed** I'm thirsty
35 **Un vaso de agua, por favor** A glass of water, please
36 **¿Qué quieres hacer?** What do you want to do?
37 **Quiero mirar la tele** I want to watch TV
38 **Quiero jugar al fútbol** I want to play soccer
39 **Quiero ir en bicicleta** I want to ride a bike
40 **Quiero nadar** I want to go swimming
41 **¿De qué color es?** What color is it?
42 **¿Cuál es tu color preferido?** What's your favorite color?
43 **Mi color preferido es el…** My favorite color is…
44 **¿Adónde vas?** Where are you going?
45 **Voy a la playa** I'm going to the beach
46 **Voy al campo** I'm going to the country
47 **Voy a la montaña** I'm going to the mountains
48 **Voy a la ciudad** I'm going to town
49 **Me pongo pantalones pequeños** I'm wearing small pants
50 **Me pongo pantalones grandes** I'm wearing big pants